ALAN RANGER

Staff Cars in Germany WW2 vol. 3

I would like to dedicate this book to my very good friend Carl Dennis (1961–2023), whose friendship I valued very much. His calm demeanour and gentle manor hid a furious passion for history, and military history in particular, He was always a great help and a fine sounding board for my efforts in this field. Carl partnered me in authoring my first ever published book on the K5e, and he also accompanied me on many enjoyable research trips to both museums and battlefields across Europe. He will be sadly missed.

Published in Poland in 2023
by Wydawnictwo Stratus sp.j.
Żeromskiego 6A,
27-600 Sandomierz, Poland
e-mail: office@wydawnictwostratus.pl

as
MMPBooks
e-mail: office@mmpbooks.biz

© Wydawnictwo Stratus sp.j.
© 2023 MMPBooks
© Alan Ranger

www.mmpbooks.biz
www.wydawnictwostratus.pl

All rights reserved. Apart from any fair dealing for the purpose of private study, research, criticism or review, as permitted under the Copyright, Design and Patents Act, 1988, no part of this publication may be reproduced, stored in a retrieval system, or transmitted in any form or by any means, electronic, electrical, chemical, mechanical, optical, photocopying, recording or otherwise, without prior written permission. All enquiries should be addressed to the publisher.

ISBN: 978-83-67227-19-3

Editor in chief
Roger Wallsgrove

Editorial Team
Bartłomiej Belcarz
Robert Pęczkowski
Artur Juszczak
Dr. Chris Lloyd-Staples

Cover concept
Dariusz Grzywacz

Book layout concept
Dariusz Grzywacz

All photos: author's collection except stated

DTP
Wydawnictwo Stratus sp.j.

PRINTED IN POLAND

Foreword

In this, the third volume on German Staff Cars I have concentrated on the Mercedes catalogue of passenger cars that saw service with the German armed forces during World War II. I have no intention of trying to provide a detailed history of the company and the car types it produced, as both have been documented before in many other worthy publications. Whilst the history of Mercedes-Benz has been written about at length many times, there are few publications that have anything more than a minimum of photos to illustrate a type. However, within my collection of German Second World War photographs I have many both interesting and intriguing previously unpublished photos that I think both the historian and modeller might find useful. As with the other volumes in the "Camera On" range, this book will concentrate on the photos of the cars as used by the German armed forces both during and before World War II, and not the history of the company and its past.

In this volume I hope to provide a more detailed impression through original photographs, taken both before and during the war, of vehicles as seen through the lens of the normal German soldier not the professional PK cameramen. The latter's well – posed shots are well known and have been published over and over again and, as such, they have already been seen by most interested parties. The following images, taken by individual soldiers, show a more personal view of the vehicles the soldiers both lived with and worked on, the views that interested the common soldier not the professional propagandist.

For the most part these photographs have been acquired via private collections and have only recently come onto the market. Most images we have used here were taken from prints made on old German Agfa paper stock and the majority of these original prints are no more than 25 mm by 45 mm in size. Whilst we have used the best quality photos from my collection, occasionally due to the interesting or rare nature of the subject matter a photo of a lesser quality has been included.

Taken during the assembly of German troops on the Polish border, this photo was taken on 29th August 1939, just two days before the invasion. The Kfz.2 Mercedes 170 VK radio-equipped *Kübelwagen* in the foreground is just part of the motorized equipment of the 6th Army that led the attack on 1st September 1939. Note the good illustration of a German railways (*Deutsche Reichsbahn*) lightweight flat bed railway car (a 5 ton load limit).

Introduction

Mercedes Benz was established as a joint venture between Daimler-Motoren-Gesellschaft and Benz & Cie that was forced on the two companies by the extreme financial predicament Germany found itself in at that time. The brand Mercedes Benz first appeared in 1924. Later the same year after Carl Benz re-joined the team and the joint venture was formalized into a full merger, forming Daimler-Benz AG. in 1926 with their first car being released for sale in the same year at the Berlin Motor Show. That car became a huge success with over 7,000 being produced in 1926 alone.

Carl Benz was born in Karlsruhe on 25 November 1844 and went on to study mechanical engineering. Once graduated he was indentured to a locksmith and rapidly proved his abilities, rapidly becoming both a designer and workshop foreman. In 1871, Carl Benz partnered with August Ritter to found his first company, the Carl Benz and August Ritter Engineering Workshop, based in Mannheim. After a falling out, the two went their separate ways and Carl Benz bought out August Ritter using his newlywed wife's dowry and managed the company on his own from 1878. His company focused its efforts on the design, development and production of two-stroke gasoline engines with a view to fulfilling Carl's dream of producing a horseless carriage (Motor Vehicle). After many months of development his gasline engine first ran successfully on New Year's Eve of 1879. Using this successful engine design as the basis to form another company, 'Gasmotorenfabrik Mannheim' (Mannheim Gas Engine Factory), in October 1882 Benz found that he could publicly float this on the market in order to secure the funds necessary to move on with his dreams of a horseless carriage. However Carl only managed to retain 5% of the total shares and as such lost control. Whilst his dream was unaltered, the majority of the board being conventional business people wished to pursue a safe business model of supplying the proven gasoline engine in its established role of a static power plant and not as the core of an illusory horseless carriage. This resulted in Carl Benz resigning from the company in January 1883.

He then moved on and formed a partnership with two other engineers, Friedrich Esslinger and Max Rose, to found the new company 'Benz & Cie. Rheinische Gasmotoren-Fabrik Mannheim' (Benz & Co. Rhine Gas Engine Factory Mannheim). This company utilized Carl's latest designs to produce the "System Benz' engine" a new much improved gasoline engine. Whilst the engine was a success, his partners did not have the same passion to develop a horseless carriage as Carl had, and did not move forward or spend enough time in its development to Carl's liking. Carl moved on again and formed yet another company with investors Julius Ganss and Friedrich von Fischer in May of 1890. Yet again the business model was to manufacture and supply static petrol engines but Carl spent a considerable amount of his time in the pursuit of his personal goal of a mobile engine. In order to finally achieve his goal of manufacturing a horseless carriage, Carl left this company and started his own company in which he had sole control, naming it "Carl Benz Söhne" (Carl Benz & Sons) in Ladenburg in 1906. Carl Benz eventually resigned as Managing Director and transfered sole management control to his sons in 1912. Late in life, now a celebrated engineer, Carl Benz took up a position on the board of directors of the new Daimler-Benz AG company, from 1926 until his death on the 4th of April 1929.

Gottlieb Daimler was born on 17th March 1834 in Schorndorf. He was apprenticed to a gunsmith based in France, earning enough to send himself to further education in Stuttgart Polytechnic in 1857 for two years. After completing contracts in both France and England he accepted the position of workshop Inspector at a Reutlingen machine tool manufacturer. It was whilst working there that he met Wilhelm Maybach in 1865. Gottlieb took the position of Technical Director for Deutz Gasmotorenfabrik, at that time a manufacturer of gasoline engines, so during his employment he became very knowledgeable in the technology of both the 2 – and 4-stroke engines. Following a long running series of disagreements with the managing director of the company Gottlieb left in 1882 to start up his own venture, working out of his Cannstatt villa with a workshop set up in his greenhouse. Here he worked on designing petrol driven four-stroke engines with Wilhelm Maybach. In 1884 they produced a successful internal combustion engine that at some point was given the nickname of the "Grandfather Clock" due to its appearance in profile, like a long case pendulum clock. The engine featured a low weight and compact design ideal for its installation into a motor vehicle. However the cost of development and construction exhausted Gottlieb's entire financial resources, forcing him to find investors/partners. In 1890 he established "Daimler-Motoren-Gesellschaft" in conjunction with Max Duttenhofer and Wilhelm Lorenz. This partnership was doomed to failure though as whilst Gottlieb wished to pursue the motor vehicle application of his engine, his new partners wanted to focus on its use as a static engine.

Wilhelm Maybach resigned from the new partnership company over what he deemed to be unacceptable terms in his contract in 1891. However unbeknown to the new members of the partnership that now ran the company, Wilhelm and Gottlieb continue to make and design engines together but listed all their new design patents in his name. The situation had a profound effect upon Gottlieb's relationship with both Max Duttenhofer and Wilhelm Lorenz, which culminated with the two of them out-voting Gottlieb Daimler in all major company decisions. This had the knock-on effect that the company lost its driving force and lost its way, finding itself in financial hardship. In the attempt to reinvigorate the company "Daimler-Motoren-Gesellschaft" (DMG) tried to re-employ Wilhelm Maybach but he refused unless Gottlieb Daimler was given control of the company. Whist this was not agreed to at first, eventually due to the ever-increasing financial pressure. DMG's situation was soon turned around, primarily by the appointment of Wilhelm Maybach as Technical Director and Gottlieb Daimler being made Inspector General of the Supervisory Board. The subsequent sales of Maybach's new Phoenix engine, that also sold well abroad with even an English industrial group of entrepreneurs offering 350.000 marks to build it under licence in the UK, saved the day. Sadly Gottlieb Daimler had little time to enjoy his newly-found and hard won position as he died of heart disease on 6 March 1900.

Wilhelm Maybach was born in Heilbronn on 9 February 1846. Sadly he was orphaned by the age of 10 with both his parents dying within 3 years of one another. Wilhelm was adopted into the Reutlinger Bruderhaus system, (a cross between an orphanage and a vocational training school). Whilst undergoing vocational training during 1864 as an engineer working in Gottlieb Daimler's machine shop, the two first met and they soon became firm friends, a friendship that would last the rest of their lives. Maybach left the company with Daimler to work at Daimler's home workshop in Karlsruhe then followed him to Deutz in 1872. Initially Maybach was employed as a draughtsman but by 1873 had been promoted to head designer. Staying by his friend's side when Gottlieb Daimler left Deutz, Maybach left with him to work together on the lightweight compact engine concept. Along with Daimler he joined the newly founded Daimler-Motoren-Gesellschaft (DMG) in November of 1890 but as previously stated he was not happy with his contract and left in February of 1891 and worked surreptitiously with Daimler to further their goals toward the production design for a horseless carriage/motorized vehicle. Funded by Daimler, Maybach and a small team worked out of the Hotel Hermann in Cannstatt, where he developed several of his engineering patents and the design of the "Phoenix" engine. Gottlieb Daimler and Wilhelm Maybach were reinstated with DMG in November 1895, due to financial pressure mostly applied by an English investment group headed by English industrialist Frederick Simms who purchased the licence to build the "Phoenix" engine. He also provided funds to enable DMG to proceed to manufacture with a number of other designs established during the time spent working in the Hotel Hermann, chiefly a belt-driven car, the first horseless carriage to be manufactured by DMG in any quantity. After the death of Max von Duttenhofer in August 1903 Maybach lost his biggest remaining supporter in the company and found himself slowly being edged out of the company's decision process and eventually, out of frustration, he resigned from DMG at the end of April 1907.

Maybach was driven to bring his designs to fruition and also provoked into doing so by the treatment he had received from DMG, so he founded his own engineering company with his sons, establishing the top of the range automotive company that bears his name to this day. Wilhelm Maybach died on 29th December 1929.

As already stated the Mercedes-Benz brand was founded in 1926, principally established upon the work of the protagonists above. The first Mercedes released by DMG was a 35hp vehicle that was predominantly designed by Wilhelm Maybach. The first Mercedes-Benz branded types were first unveiled at the Berlin Motor Show of 1926 – they were the 8/38 hp two-litre car (W 02) and the 12/55 hp three-litre model (W 03). They also introduced the now iconic three-pointed star logo on top of their radiator caps.

Mercedes-Benz went on to establish itself as a major player in Germany's automotive manufacturing industry, producing cars, trucks and buses. It had a major success with its W15 design, the car that became known as the Type 170. It was first unveiled at the Paris Motor Show of 1931 to great acclaim. The type went on to become the company's bestselling model of the 1930s.

Once the Nazis came to power in 1933 Mercedes-Benz was "encouraged" by the Nazi regime to take on other work, such as the manufacture of aero engines and military vehicles. To enable this extra work the company had to establish other factories. Mercedes-Benz during the war years had factories located in Sindelfingen and Marienfelde (the two original small manufacturing sites), purpose-built large motor vehicle plants in Untertürkheim, Sindelfingen and Mannheim and two large purpose-built Aero Engine plants built in 1936 located in Marienfelde and Genshagen, The Company's headquarters were located in Stuttgart, as they still are.

Whilst many of the different cars manufactured by Mercedes in the years prior to the beginning of WWII were commandeered, purchased or requisitioned from other civilian sources, by far the majority of the Mercedes types to see service in the role of Staff Car were of the Mercedes model V170 type, as will be seen by the number of photographs of the type in this volume 3 of my staff car trilogy. I have however also chosen to include in this publication on staff cars Mercedes' own factory military conversion of the type into a command radio car, the Sd.Kfz. 2 V170 VK, as they are also commonly seen being used as staff cars as when they are seen / photographed in service. The Sd.Kfz. 2 V 170 VK radio car was usually serving as the primary transport for a field officer of one arm of the German military or another, and sometimes even a ranking Nazi party official.

This Mercedes 170 V Type W136 2 door 4 seat cabriolet body style "B" was photographed in the Labenne area of South West France close to the town of Bayonne.

Mercedes 170 V

Mercedes 170V. Model-W136

The Mercedes 170V made its first public appearance at the Paris Motor show in February of 1936, and proved to be so popular that it became Mercedes largest selling type between 1936 and 1939 with a total of over 75,000 being built – note that figure of 75,000 is based on chassis numbers used. A further 15,000 170 chassis were used in the manufacturing of box body vans, flat bed light trucks and other specialist body types, so as can be seen by far the majority of 170V chassis finished as various body styles of the standard civilian car types. Mercedes produced the 170V from 1936 until nearly all car production was stopped by order of Hitler and production facilities turned truck production or aero engines dependent upon the production plants speciality in 1942.

Mercedes produced the following as standard:
- 2 door saloon, hard roof (Limousine/sedan) bodied car.
- 4 door saloon, hard roof (Limousine/sedan) bodied car.
- 4 door soft roof saloon (a four-door saloon with full door frames but with a with a full-length retractable/foldaway canvas roof top section.
- 2 door. 2 seat cabriolet body style "A"
- 2 door. 4 seat cabriolet body style "B"
- 2 seat covered cab with a small flatbed truck type
- 2 seat covered cab commercial variant was offered, either as a flatbed truck or with a box body (Van body) behind the cab.
- 3 seat radio military car body. That will be covered in its own section to follow.

The Mercedes 170's suffix of V referred to the engine being mounted in the front of the car, in German front is Vorn, there was a rear engined type but only small pre-production run was ever manufactured it was suffixed with the letter "H" stood for the German word Heck that translates as the stern (the rear of a boat or in this case a car). Apparently only 24 or 16 of these rear-mounted vehicles were produced, but I have not been able to confirm this from actual Mercedes records.

The Mercedes 170V was powered by a 1,700cc four cylinder petroleum engine of Mercedes own design. This engine was also a new design from 1936 and designed to replace an earlier 1700cc engine but while the old engine had 6 cylinders, the new engine with side valves was significantly more powerful and produced 37hp at 3,400 revolutions per minutes (RPM). The engine powered a four speed gear box + one reverse gear that at first only had synchromesh between the third and fourth gear, but from 1940 onwards the gear box was improved so that all gears were equipped with synchromesh. This engine and drive chain could achieve in optimal conditions 28 miles per gallon (MPG) which was quite good for the time. This proven reliability and serviceability in civilian use was also proven in military service. A staff car made the Mercedes one of the few regular civilian production cars of the time that the German armed forces purchased in some numbers direct from the manufacturer without any form of militarization, although many had military additions added during or even before their service career started. These included Notek lights, pennant flag frames and military style number plates. In conclusion, the 170V proved to be a very useful addition to the German motor pool. It did however suffer in off-road conditions that it was never intended to face, such as those found on the Eastern Front.

Opposite page: Here we have a Mercedes 170 V Type W136 2 door, 2 seat cabriolet body of style "A". This smart little 2 seater is a staff car belonging to an officer of the German Navy who was attached to an "S" Boat squadron based between both Calais and Boulogne, in the late summer of 1940. Here we see the Naval Officer sight-seeing in the now quiet and peaceful villages in the surrounding area that only a few months before were a battle field where no quarter was being given. The photo is dated 11th September 1940 and the officer in question was one Macki Barstoff, from whose album this photo came, an album I purchased many years ago in a second hand shop in Koblenz, Germany.

Mercedes 170 Cabriolet A type, and B type

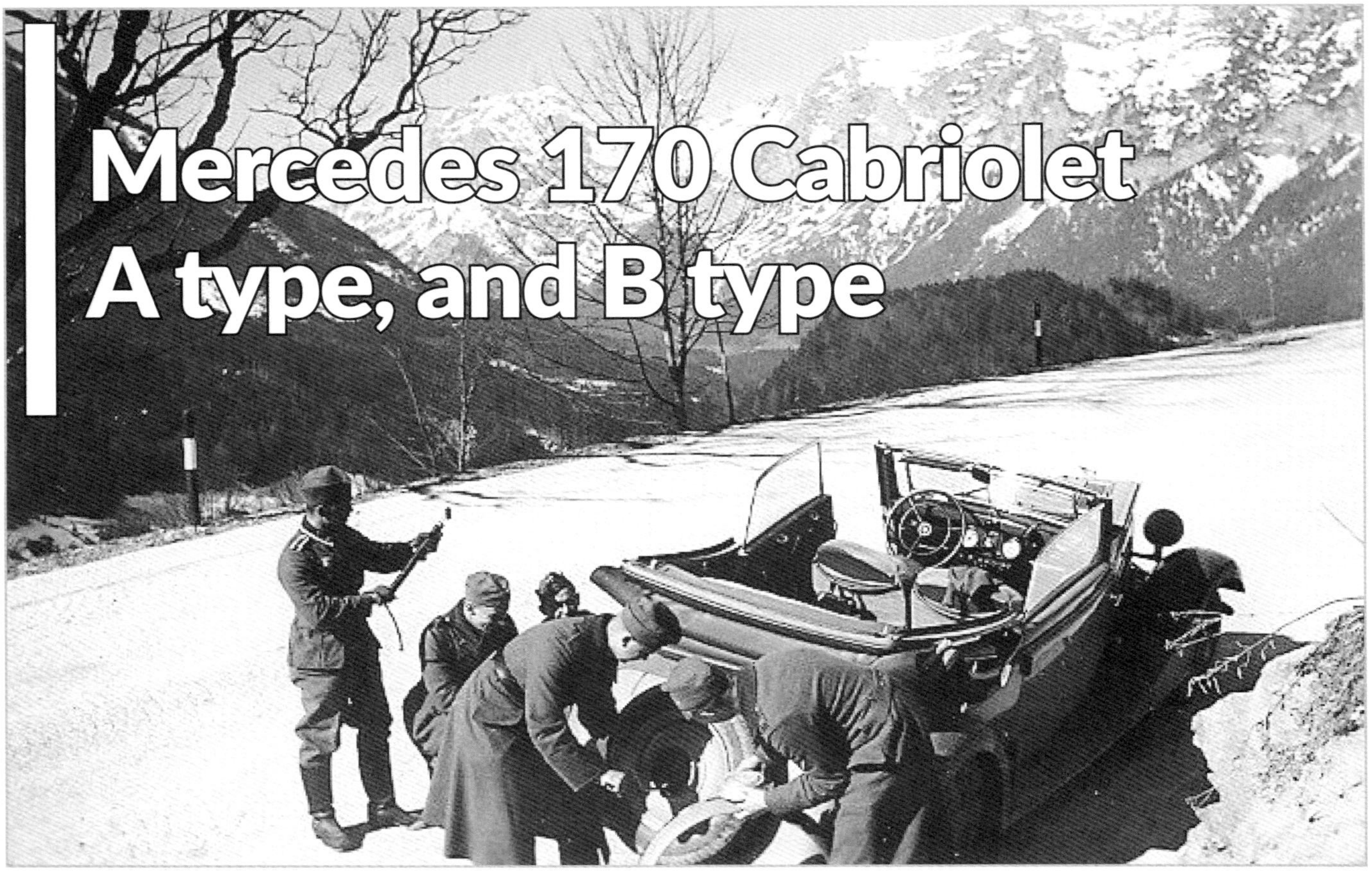

Above: This is clearly a 4-seater cabriolet Type B. By far the rarer of the two types of cabriolet taken on charge by the German military via requisitioning private vehicles from the public was the 170 V cabriolet Type "A" 2-seater, for two main reasons; one, not many were manufactured in the first place and second, it was just not viable for a car with such fuel consumption to only be able to carry a driver and one passenger for the military.

In this photo the crew and some comrades are about to change a wheel. They can be seen using the cranked spanner to undo the retaining lugs of the spare wheel while the soldier on the far left is adjusting the jack to be able to fit it under the car. Lastly note this car is still resplendent in its high gloss civilian paint finish of Gloss Black wings/fenders and running boards with Gull Grey body work and is fitted with a rare heated windscreen panel on the driver's side.

Right: This Mercedes 170 V cabriolet Type "A" 2 seater has been repainted in overall matt Panzer Grey but still retains its civilian number plate that shows that the car was originally registered in Ingolstadt City, Bavaria, as confirmed by the initial 3 letters IIN. This car is taking part in a parade celebrating the *Anschluss* (Annexation) of Austria on 13th March 1938. This parade was held in Mauerkirchen, Austria on the 15th of March just two days later. This northern part of Austria was populated by mainly German stock and welcomed the German annexation.

This nice profile view of a Mercedes 170V cabriolet type "B" 2 that belongs the NSKK (German: *Nationalsozialistisches Kraftfahrkorps*), a paramilitary wing of the Nazi party. This beautifully turned out car complete with military add-on trafficators and a Notek light, driver's side windshield heater, canvas folded down roof cover and is also sporting a NSKK pendant on the front left wing. Sadly this car belongs to the commandant of the French NSKK driving school also based at Melun, France. Collaborators who joined the NSKK were given specialist driver training. The uniform the French traitor is wearing is overall brown with a black collar and top part of the forage cap.

Bottom: A German convoy is seen using a Yugoslavian railway line to advance upon on 12th April 1941 as paved roads were in short supply in those days in Yugoslavia. The first car pictured in full is a Mercedes 170V cabriolet type "B" fitted with a Notek light but has factory incorporated trafficators fitted flush with the body panels. The car immediately behind it is an Opel 2 litre, behind that an Opel Super 6, in fact every vehicle in this photograph is of a different type – a logistical nightmare in the making.

Here we have a fine portrait view of the stylish Mercedes 170 V cabriolet type "B" 2 door 4 seater, on an street in Hanover, Germany. The car has been repainted overall Panzer Grey but still retains its civilian number plate. On the front bumper supports a triangular frame has been added that supports an extra headlight at its pinnacle. There is a canvas cover that has been placed over the folded down roof tilt, this was a civilian extra that tided up the appearance of the folded down roof but also prevented wind damage to it whilst driving at high speed. Also of interest is the spare wheel retaining clamp that is seen due to there being no spare wheel in its stowage tub on the left-hand side front wing, and also the addition of a military pattern horn. Despite this photograph being taken on 4th August 1942 there are no blackout covers on any of the headlights.

Opposite page, bottom: The crew of this 170 V cabriolet type "B" are obviously having a sort out of their equipment that they load the car up with. Note amongst this mess we can see that the car has a fascine of logs tied together with wire rolled up and stowed under the rear mounted spare wheel. This photo was taken in Russia in August of 1942 in the area covered by army group centre.

Above: Photographed on the busy streets of Leipzig, Germany on 22nd June 1940, is this 170 V cabriolet type "B" that has been fitted with the rare metal factory-fitted blackout covers for the headlights, only made by Mercedes in the last year of production of the 170 V. Note they still retain the civilian gloss black finish. The tactical symbol in white below the *Wehrmacht's* "WH" designation denotes that the car belongs to a motorised mapping detachment. Of interest are the military style trafficators fitted on the door post each side just below the windshield (a rectangular box that held a spring loaded arm with a long orange light along its bottom edge to be used as indicators, the bar would come out from the box and stand horizontally to indicate the direction of turn the driver was about to make). These were an optional extra on the civilian models but were fitted as standard once the car had been requisitioned by the military.

Opposite page, top: After getting a flat tyre this German is about to change the wheel and his companion is taking the picture from the hill side above him giving us a good view of both the engine compartment and the canvas roof (tilt top). The white square with "WH" in Panzer Grey on the left wing is unusual because it is more common to paint WH in white directly onto the surface. The tactical or unit symbol on the right hand front wing is not identifiable, but it is similar to the symbol for a vehicle belonging to a bicycle unit and it may just be a variation upon it. The circle is in Yellow and the "X" in Panzer Grey. The white letter "F" on the door is not uncommon and usually indicates vehicle motorpool's identification. However the yellow "W" on the right wing is not familiar, and the markings on this car are an oddity to be sure. The photo was taken on 16th February 1939 in the Koblenz area of Germany. Lastly note the trafficators – they are of the original factory fit type and recessed into the car's body panels.

This Mercedes 170V 2 door 4 seated cabriolet type "B" was photographed on 26th July 1942. It belonged to the 17th Army part of Army Group South, this unit was made up of German, Hungarian and Slovak troops and in this car as we can see two Germans and a Hungarian who is standing in the car. The photo was taken in the valley of the Kobyl'nya River east of Kokhanivka in central Ukraine and gives us a great view of the inner door card, its pocket and the stowage within it.

Bottom: This Mercedes 170V cabriolet type "B" is sporting a command pennant that indicates it is being used by senior *Wehrmacht* officers. The car is fitted with a third headlight in the usual way and all have a blackout cover fitted. The vehicle is painted overall Panzer Grey and of interest is the windscreen that can be seen to be in its open position, hinged along the top edge of the frame, I would have thought that the occupants would be cool enough with the top down and all the windows wound down as well but obviously not. The photo is dated August 1940 and as the album this photo comes from has other photos from this date all located in the Pas de Calais area of France I think it's safe to say this photo was taken there as well.

Above: This convoy of various types of vehicles belong to Panzer Group Kleist that was the first operational formation of several Panzer corps that the *Wehrmacht* created for the Battle of France on 1 March 1940. Field Marshal Paul Ludwig Ewald von Kleist was the group's commander and it was named after him and the group adopted the letter "K" as the group's recognition symbol. This group all belong the this battle group. The lead vehicle is a Mercedes 170V cabriolet type "B" that has a rip in the canvas tilt and a large dent in the left front wing and is not fitted with blackout covers for the headlights. The second vehicle in the convey is a 1934 pattern Opel Blitz, the third a Sd.Kfz. 10/4 with a canvas cover over the 20 mm Flak 30 gun and gun deck, it is also towing an ammunition trailer.

A fantastic photograph of an ex-civilian overall gloss black Mercedes 170V cabriolet type "B" with the optional internal trafficators fitted in the body side panels. This requisitioned vehicle still has its civilian number plate but has had a command pennant frame fitted that now has a senior officer's pennant attached and also it has had two electric military style horns attached to the front bumper either side of the radiator. Lastly it has a windshield heater that covers both the driver's side as well as the passenger's side – this must have been a top of the range Mercedes 170V and the pride and joy of some quite wealthy member of the public before it was acquired by the military. This photo was taken on a the coastal road next to the Baltic sea close to the small town of Nienhägen, Germany, on 22th July 1943. Quite how this car remains in its civilian finish this late in the war is unknown but would make an interesting story no doubt.

Opposite page, bottom: Sadly I have no background information on this photo so can't give location or time, but from what I can tell this is a remote radio listening and direction finding unit that have set themselves up in a wooden hut on a hill top,. The command/radio direction finder caravan is set up just below the brow of the hill with its masts higher than any obstruction, an ideal set up. The rear of a Mercedes 170V can be seen parked outside the hut. Note that this overall Panzer Grey car still has chrome bumpers

Bottom: Proof that officers can do physical work when the need arises. Here an officer helps his driver fold the canvas roof back neatly to prvent it billowing out and becoming torn whilst traveling at high speed. This view offers us a nice look inside the Mercedes 170V cabriolet type "B" 2 door 4 seater. The photo was taken on 9th April 1943 in Duisburg, Germany.

Opposite page top: Another photograph of a convoy led by a Mercedes 170V cabriolet type "B". This is dated 14th May 1940, a significant day as it is the very day that the Dutch surrendered. It is possible that this group have not heard the news yet and are just at a halt as no one seems to be celebrating, and indeed the driver is clearly taking a nap. This car, although painted overall Panzer Grey and with a tactical marking on its left wing, does not appear to have any mechanical changes to that of its previous civilian life. The truck the group are standing in front of is a Mercedes 3 ton towing a factory Mercedes factory supplied 1.5 ton utility trailer. Pre-war in Germany all the major suppliers offered a trailer as an option with their 3 ton trucks – Ford, Opel, Mercedes, Man etc.

Here we have an immaculately turned out Mercedes 170V cabriolet type "B" 2 fitted with one extra spot light on the lower right wing and the military add-on trafficators. It also has had its folded down roof fitted with a bespoke cover that was an optional extra from the factory, another confirmation that this is an ex-civilian car. Military orders for the Mercedes 170 did take place but only a very few were ordered direct from Mercedes, by far the majority of the staff cars we see in this volume were sourced via requisition from civilian owners. Sadly I can't find any reference to the marking on the left wing, however I can tell you the car belonged to I Gruppe KG 51 whilst they were based at Melun, France, during the "Battle of Britain". Note the blemishes on the door and elsewhere are not in the paint work but are on the actual photo print paper. I can only assume through damp over the years before I purchased the album.

Mercedes 170 Sun Roof

This Mercedes 170V 4 door saloon fitted with a sun roof, a rectangular hole in the top of the roof that goes from just behind the windscreen frame and just inboard from the door jams back to just on top of rear boot/trunk. The rear window panel is incorporated into the concertinered canvas weather proof roof sheet that can be opened from the front and pulled back to the rear on warm dry days. The car still has its civilian number plates but has been painted overall Panzer Grey. The tactical marking in Yellow just above the White "WH" indicates that this car belongs to the commander of the 1st company of a motorized Nebelwerfer Unit. Sadly the identification of the Yellow, White and Red diagonally striped shield eludes me, but this may be the symbol of LVI Panzer-Korps. The photo was taken on 1st September 1941 somewhere in western Russia.

Bottom: The driver of this this Mercedes 170V saloon fitted with a sun roof holds the rank of Obergefreiter, roughly equivalent to a full corporal in British forces. The car bears the command penant for a senior *Luftwaffe* officer and is fitted with a Notek light, add-on trafficators and a driver's side wing mirror that is attached to the door pillar. This photo was taken in in front of the Panzerhalle in *Luftwaffe* barracks in Cottbus, Germany on 4th June 1944 and yet the car is still in overall Panzer Grey.

These two soldiers with a very relaxed attitude were photographed with their very dusty sun-roofed Mercedes 170V on 23rd July 1942 somewhere in the Russian steppe – actually in the area around the northern Ukrainian town of Shostka where a large German garrison was based to guard and ensure the continued production of explosives from a large factory complex located in the town. Of note is the extra spotlight on the front bumper, the external added trafficators and that the soldier on the left of the picture is holding a signal paddle.

Another group with one of the same soldiers as above, taken at the same time in the same place, I guess. Now the soldier with the pipe seen in the top picture is taking the photograph.

Another photo of a soft-roofed Mercedes 170V being used as prop for a photo to send home. Note here the sun roof is folded fully back and the canvas cloth can be seen concertinaed up behind the door at window level and also that the door pocket is fitted with a zip fastener, a detail I have never noticed before. This photo was taken in August 1942 in the area around Avranches, France.

This soft-roofed Mercedes 170V has been painted overall Panzer Grey but still retains its chrome radiator grille and bumpers. It has however received several bumps and dents to its various front and rear wing panels. The car is fitted with a Notek light and its sunroof is fully open. Oddly this photo was taken at exactly the same place as another I have that was printed in German staff Cars Vol. 2 on page 71, showing a Opel Admiral but dated 3rd April 1942, whereas this photo was taken on 14th September that same year and comes from a totally different source.

A sad photo in many ways, as this photo shows two German officers who have stopped to have a picture taken with a small party of Belgian prisoners by some ad-hoc makeshift anti-tank barriers thrown up in desperation on the road to Kortrijk in western Belgium on 15th June 1940. The car is overall Panzer Grey with a Notek light, add-on trafficators and a command pennant frame added to the standard factory equipment.

I have a photo of my car driving through the same ford, only now it a tarmacked road near the small French village of Pont Erembourg north east of the town of Flers, France. This photo of a 4-door soft-roofed Mercedes 170V was taken on 8th November 1943. Note that the car is painted overall *Dunkel Gelb* (Dark Sand Yellow) and is fitted with a Notek light, add-on trafficators and a padded radiator screen cold weather guard. It also has a steel strip frame welded to its rear for the transportation of a 20 liter jerrycan but at the time this photo was taken no jerrycan is fitted.

A heroic shot of a 4-door soft-roofed Mercedes 170V with its roof fully open and its driver. This *Luftwaffe* car only appears to have had a Notek light and trafficators added to the original factory build and it is painted in overall Panzer Grey with white width indicator strips on both front wings and, unusually, a white panted front bumper. This photo was taken at the *Luftwaffe* barracks in Potsdam, Germany on 3rd June 1941.

This soft-roofed Mercedes 170V is still very much in its civilian guise. If it were not for the German corporal (*Obergefreiter*) sitting on the left-hand side wing its military credentials would be in doubt. The only addition is the horn and that is yet to be painted. This car still retains it's civilian number plate that show it originally was registered in the Schleswig Holstein region of Germany and its gloss black with chrome trim finish, but when the photo was taken it was in a Berlin industrial suburb during August of 1941.

Two soldiers standing next to a soft-roofed Mercedes 170V that has been painted overall Panzer Grey and been fitted with a Notek Light and the padded cold weather radiator guard. Note that the radiator guard has had its central main panel folded down and clipped in place. Lastly note that the car's headlights have been fitted with the rare cloth headlight blackout covers (common on many cars but rarely seen on Mercedes). Sadly I have no other information on this photo as to its when and where.

This Berlin registered soft-roofed Mercedes 170V is seen in Koblenz Germany on 25th July 1941. It has been painted overall Panzer Grey but other than that has no military additions at all, bar the crew and it tactical symbol that is in red painted on the left-hand wing and denotes the car belongs to a Motorized Railway Engineer Company. Also note the white "WH" has not had the cross bar added to the "H" as yet, an odd omission. Lastly note the very good view here of the factory-fitted trafficators mounted flush with the car's bodywork just in front of the door handle and in the base of the A pillar – and how old is that boy, surly not the driver?

Another soft-roofed Mercedes 170V seen here on a residential street in Duisburg Germany on 27th January 1943. The driver holds the rank of Gefreiter roughly the equivalent of a British lance corporal. The car has been painted overall Panzer Grey and has had a Notek light, windshield heater on the driver's side, command pennant frame and pendent fitted, as well as a cold weather padded radiator guard. But most interesting of all is the metal Nazi Eagle badge that has been attached to the radiator grille and is seen through the folded down radiator grille guard, I have never seen that addition before.

A nice over view of a soft-roofed Mercedes 170V with its folding roof open and oddly its rear seat cushion hung over the rear of the back seat. Note this Panzer Grey car has had a Notek light and trafficators added to it, but still retains its chrome radiator grille and both front & rear chromed bumpers. This photo was taken on 2nd June 1943 in Makarska in the Independent State of Croatia, as it was then. It was incorporated into Yugoslavia after the war.

Above, left: Another Berlin-registered soft-roofed Mercedes 170V, this one is in overall Panzer Grey and it has add-on trafficators and a Notek light. Other than that it is unremarkable. Seen on a Berlin street in May 1941.
Above, right: This soft-roofed Mercedes 170V is in the French barracks of Sudan that were taken over by the Germans following the fall of France. The car is seen in the winter of 1941/42 on the parade ground of the base. Note the Notek light, the command pennant frame and pendant, and that the bumpers are still chrome and unpainted

A nice photo of the crew and their soft-roofed Mercedes 170V seen in a Berlin suburb on 24th May 1940. This car has had no military additions at all not even a repaint. The colour scheme is one of the factory's standards of gloss black chassis and wings with gloss red bodywork and chrome trim. Even the padded radiator cold weather guard is of the civilian pattern. I can only surmise that the car has only just been requisitioned and is yet to be militarized, as I doubt such a standout vehicle would be allowed to serve in the military even in a second line role in such a loud and brash colour scheme. Lastly note the patterned road cobbles, this was a common feature of large European cities before the war.

A very dirty soft-roofed Mercedes 170V seen in a Dutch timber yard located in the Harlingen coastal area. The text relating to this photograph in the album indicates that this *Luftwaffe* officer was in the process of acquiring timber for use in a radar installation site that was being constructed close by. Other than the paint job of overall Panzer Grey and the retrofitted trafficators, no other military additions are visible on this car. The photo was taken in May of 1941.

This rather tired looking soft-roofed Mercedes 170V is photographed in France somewhere in the Le Havre area on 23rd July 1943. This car has a damaged sun roof as can be seen, exposing the framework beneath. It is part open and in a dishevelled state, the mechanic looks to have been interrupted by the female now seated in the car whilst he was doing something to the rear axle area of the car. The rear wheel has been removed and the car is elevated by the bottle jack seen fitted to the jacking point under the "B" pillar between the doors under the running board. I have no information as to what was going on here or to the relationship of the couple pictured but can state that the white tactical symbol on the left front wing denotes that the car belongs to a Signal Company and the small number 1 under it means that it is part of the first troop. Oddly the *Wehrmacht* "WH" is in Yellow.

Amongst my collection of photographs I have 7 photos of various vehicles next to this landmark, but infuriatingly I have no clue as to what and where it was or is. Obviously it has something to do with wine production but I have no information on it. If any one does I would like to ask them to contact the publisher with the information. Parked outside the monument is a soft-roofed Mercedes 170V in overall Panzer Grey and it was photographed on 2nd October 1941, but as I said sadly I do not know where.

Bottom: This soft-roofed Mercedes 170V unsurprisingly enough has its folding roof firmly closed on this cold and snowy January day of 1942 in the area around Lublin, Poland. This Mercedes is in overall Panzer Grey and has a heated widescreen unit that covers both the driver's and passenger's sides and a padded cold weather shield over the radiator grille that has its central panel folded half way down and cloth blackout headlamp covers. It has Yellow number 8 on the left wing and a white tactical symbol on the right wing but I can't see enough of to identify it correctly.

Mercedes 170 Limousine

Above: This is a brand new Mercedes 170V Limousine photographed outside the beautiful art deco doors of the Berlin exhibition hall located in Berlin Westerland. Although this is not a staff car as yet I have included it as it is such a good photograph of the type.
Bottom: A nice view of the upper side of a Mercedes 170V Limousine that has been requisitioned into the *Wehrmacht* as indicated by the White "WH" above a tactical symbol that indicates that this car belonged to a construction unit. Other than the white "WH" and the tactical symbol this car is still in the same finish that it was when requisitioned, gloss black with chrome trim. The photo was taken in March of 1943 but I have no location.

Above: This typical hero shot for the type to send home was taken in Frankfurt on 24th March 1941. The Mercedes 170V Limousine is being used as a prop by its driver, an *Unterfeldwebel* (*Luftwaffe* rank equivalent to a British Sergeant). The car itself is fitted with a Notek light, the unidentified unit marking is red circle with an outer white ring and white number "6" in the red circle's top left quarter.
Bottom: Walking towards the cameraman, this *Luftwaffe Kornettenhapitan* (Lieutenant Commander) does not look too happy to be photographed. His Mercedes 170V Limousine behind him is painted overall Panzer Grey and has add-on trafficators, a Notek light and a command pennant frame with pennant fitted. The flag painted on the right-hand wing is a variation on a *Luftwaffe* Regiment Command flag. A three colour horizontal band with a Nazi spread eagle in its centre, the wing of which were in the top band and the laurel wreath with its swastika was in the central band. This flag appears to be Yellow, Black, Yellow, with a silver eagle.

Above: A *Luftwaffe* Officer is having his Mercedes 170V Limousine refuelled by his driver. The car had a tubular shaped tank mounted at the top of the fire wall right at the back of the engine compartment. The car is painted Panzer grey but still retains it chrome bumpers and radiator grille – not that they are going to give the car away covered In the amount of dirt and dust we see here. This photo was taken on the outskirts of Babruysk, a city that is now in Belarus, in the summer of 1941.

Bottom: Taken in Leipzig, Germany, in the spring of 1944 this Mercedes 170V Limousine appears to be painted in *Dunkel Gelb* (Dark Sand Yellow) judging by the tonal difference between the car and the tone of the officer's uniform seen behind the car.

Photographed in Norway during July of 1944, this Mercedes 170V Limousine has a Notek light and factory-fitted trafficators. The Panzer Grey overall paint scheme is highlighted by the contrasting white painted wing outer edges both front and rear, with both sets of bumpers painted white as well. The very rare and unusual tactical symbol on the door is that of a Ministry of the *Wehrmacht* vehicle assigned to the department of civil engineering.

Bottom: This Mercedes 170V Limousine fitted with a Notek light is painted in overall *Dunkel Gelb* (Dark Sand Yellow). The mechanic in his Black Panzer Corps uniform is looking at some problem with the engine, the fuel tank we have seen being refilled previously can be clearly seen here above the engine against the fire wall. Note the engine compartment has not been repainted and is still in gloss black, the original factory finish. The tactical symbol on the left-hand wing painted in red indicates that this car belonging to Armoured Headquarters Company.

Another overall Panzer Grey Mercedes 170V Limousine. This car has had a Notek light, command pennant frame and senior officer's pennant fitted. The photograph was taken in the garage block of the senior officers' barracks, part of the military complex in Munster, Germany in May 1943. The tactical symbol above the White "WH" on the left-hand wing is that of the commander of a non-motorised supply train. The same car is shown below.

The joys of a home posting, this Mercedes 170V Limousine is parked in the garden of a senior officer next to his deck chair! The photo was taken on 3rd June 1940 in Dortmund, Germany. The car is fitted with both a Notek light and a command pennant frame with senior officer's pennant mounted in it; the tactical symbol that is painted in Yellow above the white "WH" marking is that of a car from the HQ's vehicle park of a non-motorised supply unit.

This Mercedes 170V Limousine belongs to the German military police. Its driver stands smoking a cigar next to his pride and joy, his uniform is that of an officer in the military police. The car has no markings whatsoever and the only way we know for sure it has been taken on charge by the military is that it has been repainted in Panzer Grey and the civilian number plate has been retained, with only the licencing region's code letters being painted over. No military add-ons have been fitted.

Below: Here we have a Mercedes 170V Limousine in overall Panzer Grey. The only military additions are the two electrical horns and a pennant flag pole flying enamelled metal Brigade Command pennant, and the also a tactical marking in white on the right-hand wing. The command Pennant indicates that the vehicle is from the Brigade's Headquarters. The driver is a Wehrmacht Gefreiter roughly the equivalent of a British lance corporal. This photo was taken on 9th February 1940 in Munich, Germany.

Above: Photographed in the winter of 1939/40 this Mercedes 170V Limousine is parked outside a café in Essen, Germany. The two crew are having a relaxed moment before moving on. The car is in overall Panzer Grey but retains it chrome bumpers. It has add-on trafficators, two electric horns and the rarer waxed cloth headlight blackout covers. The car has the usual white painted "WH" on the right-hand wing and a white tactical marking on the left-hand wing, denoting the car as belonging to an a horse-drawn supply column (*Kolonne* 4). The letters denote the individual unit within the regiment.

This Mercedes 170V Limousine is as it left the factory, apart from its Panzer Grey paint scheme. It has the rarer waxed cloth headlight covers and a padded radiator cover. However the main point of interest here is the artwork on the car's right-hand wing – it appears to have a rough front view of the Basillque de Sacre-Coeur in Paris France, painted in white above a large yellow painted roman number three with the "WH" next to it but smaller. On the left-hand wing is a yellow number 23 that is the car's pool number. This car is part of the German Paris garrison's motor pool and was photographed on 3rd May 21942

Opposite page, bottom: Leading this column of vehicles from a signal company is a Mercedes 170V Limousine that has stopped due to overheating and the rest of the convoy is taking the opportunity for a short rest break. The car still retains its civilian number plate and other than the Panzer Grey Paint paint and the situation it has been photographed in there is nothing to indicate it is indeed a Military vehicle. It carries the tactical symbol for a signals unit on its left-hand wing above the "WH" *Wehrmacht* symbol, both painted in white. The truck immediately behind the Mercedes is a 1934 pattern Opel Blitz and this whole convoy was photographed on 20th June 1940, somewhere in the Pas de Calais, France, during the time of the Dunkirk evacuations.

Seen in Belgium in June 1940 in the area around the town of Zottegem is this Mercedes 170V Limousine in overall Panzer Grey, fitted with just a Notek light with no other military additions. The badge on the side is a generic *Luftwaffe* badge of a black shield with a Yellow border surround and a white silhouette of diving Ju 87 "Stuka". The badge on the left-hand wing is also generic, it is the same as the German shield found on both *Wehrmacht* and *Luftwaffe* steel helmets. I can't identify any particular unit that owned this car but still with the markings it has on show and its missing front bumper it's an interesting subject. Note the crew's tent made from individual soldier's ponchos buttoned together on the right–hand edge of the photo.

Bottom: This proud driver stands in front of his charge, a very dusty Mercedes 170V Limousine painted in overall Panzer Grey. It is fitted with a Notek light, add-on trafficators, a full width windscreen heater and a padded cold weather radiator grille cover. The most interesting feature of this Mercedes is the headlight covers that are of the factory fitted style of domed steel disc with the blackout cut-out in it held in place by the headlight lamps lens retaining ring. However the unusual thing here is that the domed cover is still in civilian gloss black and the retaining ring is still in its chrome plated finish. I am surprised that neither the cap or ring have ever been repainted. Lastly the car also retains its original front and rear bumpers, both still in their original chrome plated finish.

Mercedes 170 Kübelwagen

This Mercedes 170 VK *Kübelwagen* in immaculate condition is parked on a roadside somewhere in the Oberhausen area of Germany on 3rd April 1941. Its radio equipment, a Fu.11 SE 100 transmitter and a Torn. Fu.d2 receiver, can be seen clearly through the side windows. Note none of the standard issued field equipment is fitted to the vehicle, not uncommon when a vehicle is being used well behind the lines in an area where roads are metalled and in good order.

Mercedes 170 VK Kübelwagen

I have included the Mercedes 170VK radio car in this volume number 3 of German Staff cars as whilst it was indeed a radio communication vehicle and not intended to be used as a staff car, it was often pressed into use as a staff car whilst on its military service. Many a senior field officer was happy to use one as a personal car as it gave all the comfort and reliability of the standard 170V cabriolet. It also came with the inherent military advantage of being able to be used to relay orders without the need of a separate radio communications vehicle.

The Mercedes 170VK utilized the same chassis as the standard 170V four-door cabriolet body version of the car, but its body was of military design and was largely made up of flat stamped steel body panels. Only the engine bonnet and the front wings/fenders were retained from the 170V car's standard body design. The 170VK had three doors: a front and rear door on the left-hand side (Drivers side) and only the front door on the right-hand side. This is because the right rear seat and door space was taken up by the radio equipment.

The Mercedes 170VK (the "K" suffix to the 170V stood for *Kübelwagen*) was manufactured from 1938 until production ended in 1942 along with all other car types made in Germany that were not fully intended for military service from their initial design. Mercedes produced over 19,000 of these vehicles which made it the second most highly produced German lightweight open-topped military car of the period.

The top two photographs on this page are of a Mercedes 170 VK *Kübelwagen* Kfz. 1 four seater with no radio equipment fitted. This was the rarer version of the car than that fitted with radios (the Kfz. 2), as a smaller number of the production of the 170VK was built in this form. The photos were taken on 23rd March 1938 in the Mercedes factory complex.

The same Mercedes as seen above but here viewed from the right front quarter. Of interest on this brand new car are the polished steel running boards obviously taken from the civilian production stock, as I am sure they would have been painted before the vehicle was issued to the troops or very soon after. Running boards were deleted on later production cars in the VK series.

A nice study of a Mercedes 170 VK Kfz. 2 with the radio cabinet fitted and its wet weather canvas tilt down and folded neatly on the rear deck. Note the spare wheels and their stowage positions in the front wings have been deleted on this model. . This photo was taken in Holland in the Utrecht area during September of 1940.

Seen in Greece in the late summer of 1941 is this Kfz. 2 Mercedes 170VK radio car, parked on a road above the site of a wrecked British 25lb field artillery piece and its totally smashed up prime mover. The Kfz. 2's crew are looking over the scene. Whatever destroyed the field piece must have been powerful as the gun's very heavy and strong positioning base and traverse ring that was usually carried under the gun carriage, on the limber or on the towing vehicle has been blown off and is now seen bent and sitting on top of the gun trail.

This *Luftwaffe* Kfz. 2 is parked right outside a *Panzerhalle* that was part of the Frankfurt Main military complex and was photographed on 27th September 1942. Of note is the radiator cold weather padded cover and the *Luftwaffe* squadron badge painted on the front doors on both sides, as I have another view (albeit badly damaged) of this same car in my collection. The *Luftwaffe* squadron badge (emblem) looks to me to be that of KG 30 but it might be 1N/JG 2's emblem instead. I leave the final choice to the *Luftwaffe* aficionados as the angle the photo was taken from makes it hard to tell.

Above: Here we have one of the 4 door Mercedes 170 VK *Kübelwagen*s without a radio fit and we can also see that this is an early production model as it has running boards fitted. This photo was taken in Greece but sadly I have no date for it, but it was probably taken in the summer of 1941. Of note is the motorcycle dispatch rider standing on the right of the photo in his motorcycle long waxed cotton coat. Two motorcycle front wheels are just visible on the edge of the photo. The troops all belong to a reconnaissance element of the XI Panzer group.

Bottom: Seen in the Calvados region of France during the late summer of 1942 is this Mercedes 170VK in overall Panzer Grey with no visible markings other than the name "Stroch" written in white along the top of the bonnet (engine cover panel). Other points of interest are the canvas headlamp covers and the distinctly unmilitary appearance of the whole scene. Three German soldiers with a very casual appearance, two standing and one seated on a hay bale making a role-up cigarette, their tent erected beside a hay-stack. A record player playing a record whilst it is seated on top of the car's bonnet, along with its associated record collection box, a soft toy dog tucked into the gap between the radiator and the front bumper and a white enamelled tea-pot/kettle rested upon the right hand wing. Even a cow bell tied to the car by a cord around the radiator filler cap. Lastly note the number plate has been whited out.

A Beautiful portrait of a Mercedes 170 VK Kfz. 2/40 light maintenance vehicle (*kleiner Instandsetzungskraftwagen*) with oxy-acetylene cylinders clearly visible in the locker. This car was photographed amongst the dock buildings of the port of Genoa Italy from where much of the supplies for Rommel's North African campaign were shipped from. Note the car is already painted in Desert Yellow over its original Panzer Grey and is in as new condition yet a custom framework has been attached to the wing for the stowage of a 20 litre Jerry can on top and in front of the spade stowage position.

Bottom: Here we have a nice front view of a Luftwaffe Mercedes 170 VK Kfz. 2 in the snow with its crew standing next to it for a group photo. The photo was taken in Northern Holland on 10th February 1943, somewhere near Leeuwarden. Of interest here are white-painted outer edges of the lower wings and the Unit/squadron badge painted on the passenger's side wing. Whilst I can't make it out, I can state that it is red shield with a Yellow symbol emblazoned upon it.

A nice portrait of a 4 door Mercedes 170 VK *Kübelwagen* (without radio) that belongs to a *Luftwaffe* unit stationed in the Pas de Calais, France, probably JG 26 based at La Touquet. This actual building has been converted to flats and can be found in the village of Wissant and it is still much the same but with a new coat of white paint and blue shutters. Note the car has been fitted with a "Notek" light on the left-hand side wing (fender) and also note the separate window panels for both the front and rear side windows that fit into the door sills and under the roof tilt. The clear parts of these side panels were made of an early acrylic type material and was very susceptible to UV degradation so they did not last long without going opaque, yellowish and also becoming brittle and cracking. This type of window was common on many German soft skins for use in side panels and consequently that is why you rarely see soft skin vehicles in the latter stages of the war with them fitted. As the clear parts of the panels became broken so the whole side panel was discarded.

Opposite page, bottom: Taken in Gent, Belgium on 5th September 1942, this Kfz. 2 radio car sits resplendent in the town square. Note that this Panzer Grey Mercedes has not got its door fitted, the doors on these *Kübelwagen*s were held in place by bar hinges with no top fastening, so by just pulling the door upwards they could be removed. Again it is not uncommon to see doors actually missing on these vehicles, as if they became damaged they also would often just be discarded. However, looking at the relatively pristine nature of this car, I would assume that they have merely been removed for ease of access and are somewhere about to be refitted as and when required.

This photo, supposedly in Norway in 1944, but likely much earlier, shows how second line units had to make do and mend and become creative with the use of their slender supply of equipment. The uniforms are of 1940 pattern, with dark collars and long boots, and a distinctly pre-war helmet pattern. This Pak 36/37 has a Mercedes 170VK 4 door *Kübelwagen* employed as its prime mover, hardly a suitable vehicle for the task. However that said the gun itself could also be called unsuited to its intended task in 1944! Lastly note that neither the Pak nor car have been repainted in *Dunkelgelb* RAL (*Reichs-Ausschuß für Lieferbedingungen*) No. 7028. Indeed, the car is in pre-war *Reichswehr* colours. This was not uncommon in second line units and much equipment was never repainted as per the orders.

As an aside, over the years I have collected many original paint chips of *Dunkelgelb* and not one is exactly the same shade as any of the others. I have heard and read so much ill-informed discussion as to the exact shade of this colour, so I will merely add this. The paint was supplied to units in tubes not unlike large toothpaste tubes that we use today, then mixed/thinned down in whatever was to hand. Dependent upon how clean the vessel was, or what had been used as the thinner (water, petrol, etc.) the colour would change. As the pigments were not of such a stable quality in the 1940's, they also suffered quickly from UV degradation, and again the shade would change. I have seen it on actual vehicles looking like a very light brown to a light greenish yellow – all are correct! Wartime descriptions often describe it as a 'mushroom soup' appearance!

Above: Here we have a very dusty Panzer Grey Mercedes 170 VK Kfz 2/1 telephone vehicle equipped with cables, switchboard and phones, seen somewhere on the Russian steppe in the late summer of 1941. Note the stowed cable guiding poles along the side of the car and that the crew are using the roof to dry out their ponchos that they slept under the night before. Lastly note that here we see the rear side window panel fitted but not the front one. This is not uncommon and was totally down to crew preference. One of the crew members is seated on a 20 litre jerry can that has a custom made stowage rack fitted to the left hand front wing.

Proof, if proof were needed, that it was not always muddy in Russia – in fact the hot, dry summers turned the steppe into a dust bowl in many areas. Here we see a very high quality view of a 3 door Panzer Grey Mercedes 170 VK Kfz. 2/1 *Fernsprechwagen*, field telephone equipped vehicle, photographed on 23rd July 1942 in the area around Oryol Oblast, Russia. That would make this car part of Army Group Centre, but sadly I have not been able to identify the Unit/ tactical symbol on the right front wing. Note the absence of the wire-guiding rods that are used to feed out the telephone line while the car is being driven along. They would normally be stowed in the two brackets seen on the rear of the right-hand side body panel. Also missing is the right-hand side headlamp blackout cover. This car also has a command pennant, fitted in a wire frame mounted on the left-hand wing/fender. This is unusual for a signals car. I think it safe to assume that this *Fernsprechwagen* car is currently being used purely as a staff car.

Opposite page, bottom: Another dusty Panzer Grey Mercedes 170 VK Radio car but this one is seen taking a sight-seeing trip around the remains of Dunkirk, France, in August 1940 a couple of months after the evacuation. As can be seen the clean-up is under way and the roads have been swept of loose debris and neat piles remain to be removed. Of interest on this car is the log fascine that is lying across the rear deck under the canvas tilt. It was a rarity to see such fancies during operation "Case Yellow", the invasion of the France and the low countries of 1940, but an almost ubiquitous accessory of all ex-civilian wheeled vehicles following the first few months of operation "Barbarossa", the invasion of Russia. Note that on the later production cars such as this one, the spare wheel tub in the left-hand side only had been deleted and a normal shaped wing/fender installed instead. Note, sometimes a spare wheel & tyre were still carried on the right-hand side/passenger's side.

Taken during May of 1943 in the suburbs of Kyiv, Ukraine (then part of Russia but hopefully never to be so again), this Kfz. 2 Mercedes radio car is parked for a quick rest break during its journey, giving time for this photo to be taken. This Panzer Grey car is well covered with dust yet the large white width markings painted on each wing remain easily visible. The car still has its winter cold weather radiator padded cover fitted to the grille but the central removable panel has been folded down and clipped in that position.

Below: This Kfz. 2 photographed on 2nd April 1943 may well be the same car as pictured above as it came from the same album that was put together by a member of the 9th recognisance battalion of the 4th Panzer Army. Seen here the fitting of the vehicle's protective windshield cover, this canvas cover also served as an anti-glare panel to aid in concealing the car from the air. Lastly note the oversized truck type wing mirror on the windshield post on the driver's side and the driver's rifle in the rear seat's travel lock to make more room for his knees in the front.

Another Kfz. 2 from the same unit as the last two photographs but definitely a different car. This time note the position of the tyre pressure white lettered stencil on the front wing is in a totally different place. Also note here the stowage of the shovel on the left wing and the single side window panel fitted to the right rear side body panel where a door would have been if this were a 4 door Kfz. 1. This side panel was often seen to be left fitted on its own on Kfz. 2s, I assume to give a little more protection to the rear of the radio sets and, as it was by the radio sets in the rear and not in any of the crew members way, it was just left there.

Seen during a "Familie's Day" at the Hanover combined service barracks on 7th July 1939. "Family Day" were encouraged by the Nazi regime as it all fed in to their "one nation, one people's army" philosophy that encouraged the people to think of the army as an extension of their family. These public events were common all over Germany and open to all members of the public, indeed the public was strongly (forcibly) encouraged to attend. Questions would be asked as to why your family did not attend if you were not there.

Here we see a Mercedes Kfz. 1 stopped for lunch on a November day in Russia during 1943. Note the thick cardboard box wedged in on top of the left wing that had been used to place lunch in. Often, due to the lack of a thermos, soldiers would use an old box, fill it with paper or straw, and use it to transport a hot meal, soup or goulash type stew contained in their mess tins, in order to keep the food warm. Of note here is that the car is fitted with all of its wet weather window panels and its canvas tilt is raised. Also note the poorly-fitting front window panel as witnessed by the visible gap – this was a common fault of this type of window arrangement.

A fully covered up Mercedes Kfz. 2 and its smiling crew member having his photo taken whilst posing next to his car. Note he is wearing a civilian-type knitted jumper that he had just received in a package from home on 20th January 1941. The note on the back of the photo tells us it was taken behind the cook house, but sadly I have no clue as to where that cook house was.

These Mercedes 170V van bodies are all factory-built as ambulances and are brand new. Seen here in the parking lot outside the factory awaiting delivery. This photo was taken on a sunny day in late October 1938. Note the white bodies and black chassis and mud guards and that these ambulances have not been fitted with hub caps.

This Kfz. 2/2 Radio van with a wooden body was based on a standard Mercedes 170VK chassis, however the bodies of such vehicles was sub-contracted out to a number of different coachworks throughout Germany. According to the text on the rear of the photo the crew borrowed a car jack and were using it to try and get this radio van out of the mud it had become stuck in. The photo was taken in the east of Holland on 29th December 1940 in the Enschede area. Note the Mercedes wooden box van type were split into 2 categories, the Kfz. 2/1 *Fernsprechwagen* (telephone van) and the Kfz. 2/2 Funkwagen (radio van).

What looks to be a maintenance unit's conversion of a standard ex-civilian Mercedes 170 salon to a Kfz. 2/2 radio van. The wooden shed type structure has been quite nicely mated up to the cut-back roof of the saloon with the addition of a flange plate to fill any gaps. The roof is higher than normal and is pitched rather than domed but these are just aesthetics, no doubt the conversion works. The frame aerial looks to be from a Horch Kfz. 19. This car was photographed on 23rd October 1943 in the Bruges area of Belgium.

This very clean, indeed new-looking, wooden bodied van is a Mercedes 170 VK Kfz. 2/2 radio van that belongs to the *Luftwaffe*; the photo was taken in the area just east of Le Havre, France, on 26th February 1942. The relaxed crew are not seen to be wearing any form of weapon be it sidearm or bayonet. Note also the total lack of blackout covers for the head lights with no Notek light fitted either and the cold weather matted screen still fitted on the radiator grille, a remnant of the just passed winter. This van is also unusually fitted with two horns, that can be seen one under each head light, and a command pennant frame mounted on its left wing/fender.

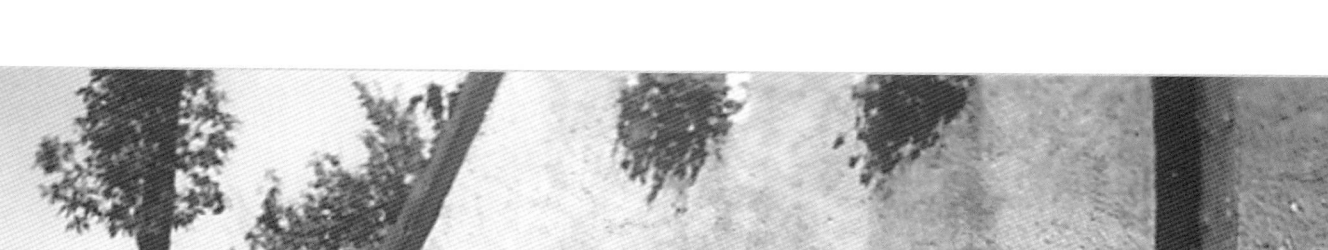

Here we have a Horch 830 R *Kübelwagen* in the foreground but the there is an interesting Mercedes Kfz. 2/2 radio van in the background. It is clearly painted in a two colour camouflage scheme of Panzer Grey and a Dark Green, although it looks lighter compared to the Panzer Grey seen here. Note the windscreen has been opened for ventilation and is hinged along its top edge. This photograph was taken on 26th August 1940 in the Angers area of France.

* The Horch Type 830 R will be covered in a future volume of German Staff Cars that will cover all four of the German car brands that were amalgamated to become Auto-Union

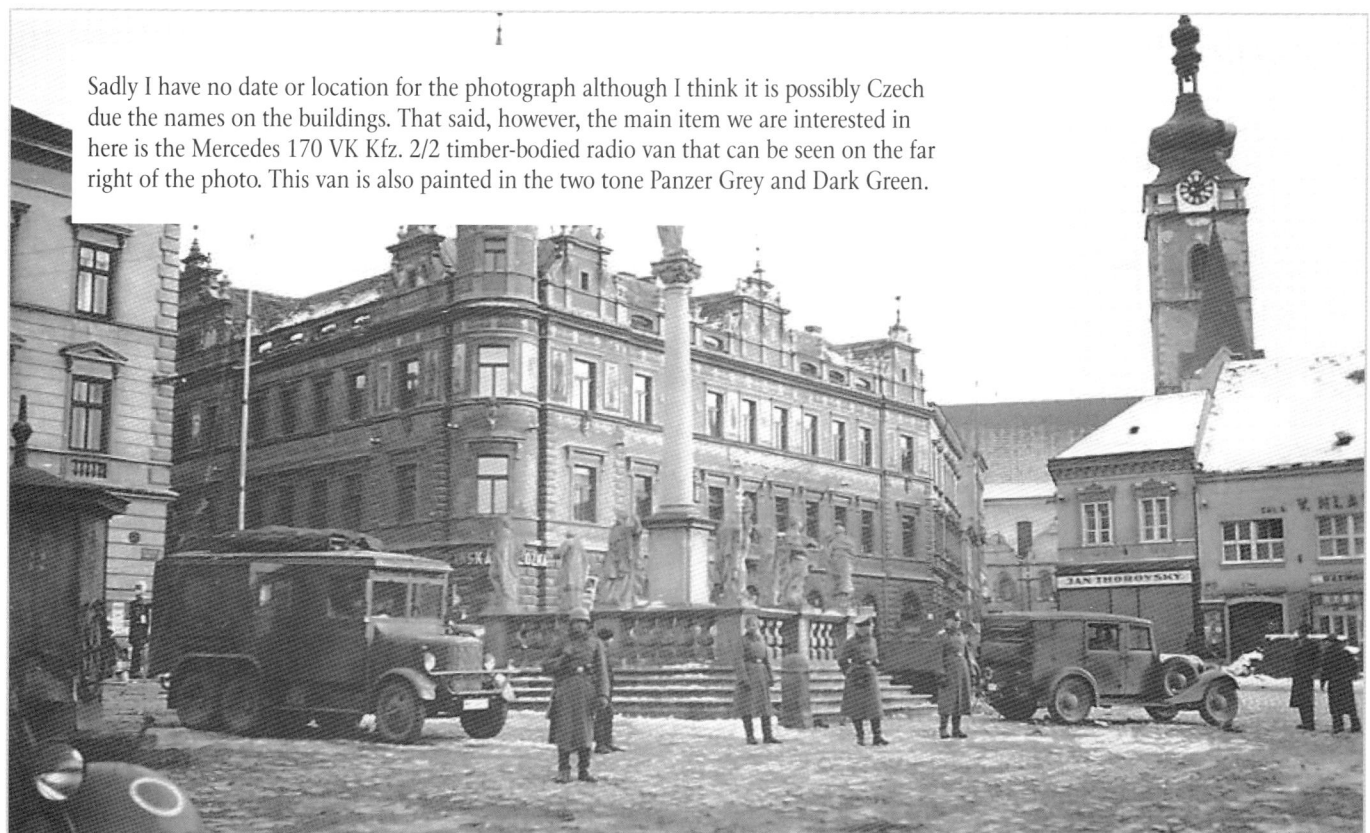

Sadly I have no date or location for the photograph although I think it is possibly Czech due the names on the buildings. That said, however, the main item we are interested in here is the Mercedes 170 VK Kfz. 2/2 timber-bodied radio van that can be seen on the far right of the photo. This van is also painted in the two tone Panzer Grey and Dark Green.

Mercedes 200, 230 & 260

Due to the similarity of many of the Mercedes types and by definition usually only having one view to try to recognise the various cars, sometimes it is not possible to positively identify the type from two or more similar looking models. In these cases I have tied it down to type as close as I can, but if the view I have to work with only enables me to narrow the identification down, I will list the versions it might be, and leave it up to those better versed in the vagaries of various Mercedes types. That said, I have identified this car as a type W143 Mercedes 230, a 4-door 4-seat saloon with a sun roof that is partly open. This Panzer Grey car has a white "WH" on the right wing and an infantry regiment tactical symbol on the left-hand wing, also in white. This photo was taken on 5th July 1943 in Marseille, France, outside an officer's club set up in a commandeered villa.

This Mercedes I have identified as a type W21 Mercedes 260 due to the car's length, it is a four door 4-seat saloon with a sun roof. Sadly I have no further information on this photo but we can identify the railway coach as belonging to SNCF, the French railway company. The colour of the car is overall Panzer Grey.

Mercedes 200, 230 & 260

The Brand name Mercedes-Benz was launched at the 1926 Berlin Motor show and it, along with its new three pointed star logo, were proudly displayed on the first two new car types manufactured by the brand – one a 2-litre and other a 3-litre engined type. The 2 litre 8/38 hp 200 model was by far the most popular and its sales in 1927 outnumbered the total sales of all the cars manufactured by all the newly merged companies that formed Mercedes-Benz put together had sold the previous year.

It was the normal practice for all cars in those days to be listed by the number of valves in the engine and the maximum horse power the engine could produce. From 1927 the engine's cubic capacity was added with it value divided by 10 i.e. a 2 litre engine 2000cc would be listed as 200 hence the Mercedes model number 8/38 hp 200 describes a car with 8 valves, 38 horse power and a 2 litre/2000cc engine. At the next year's Berlin motor show, Mercedes for the first time gave a car a name and launched that years 1928 model of the 8/38 hp 200 as the 200 Stuttgart and the 3 litre as the 260 Stuttgart, a masterful marketing stroke at the time such that now all cars have names and we think nothing of it.

Whilst the history of the early Mercedes-Benz cars is interesting, it is not the subject I am concentrating on here – but it should be noted that a very few a very few of these early cars were still requisitioned in to the military in 1939 along with many other types that had been the preserve of the civilian motorist. However in 1934 Mercedes began to supply the German Reichswehr with a car based on their 260 Stuttgart car's chassis with bucket seats, open-sided simplified body style and solid disc steel wheels rather than the civilian model that was equipped with spoked wheels. Its designation was simply listed as the Stuttgart 260 *Kübelwagen*. It proved to be a highly regarded vehicle by the military of the time due to its ruggedness and ease of maintenance. Although a rarity by 1940, a small number were still to be found in service on all fronts. The Stuttgart 260 *Kübelwagen* was in production from August 1934 until December of 1935 with a total of 1507 being produced, manufacturing of the body work was mostly carried out in Sindelfingen plant. However the vehicle was also produced by Trutz of Coburg and Gaubschat in Berlin. In total, the standard passenger versions of the 8/38 produced was 9,105 along with 6452 of all versions of the Stuttgart 200 and 6757 of all versions of the Stuttgart 260. When compared to present days car plant manufacturing totals, these numbers appear small. However back in the 1930's this was a large number when compared to other European car companies of the time.

Even though such unit volumes may appear modest by today's standards, the W 6506 / W 02 / W 11 model family achieved considerable success in its market segment. All three models were manufactured in Stuttgart-Untertürkheim. Anyone referring today to the Stuttgart model will normally mean the entire model family, even though this name was introduced until the facelift in autumn 1928.

This car I have identified as a type W143 Mercedes 230 as it is a 2 door 4 seater cabriolet. It looks to be a *Luftwaffe* car as the troops in it are *Luftwaffe* personnel. Note the wooden fascine lodged in-between the engine compartment cover and the left-hand wing, the bread bag and the water bottle hanging on the inside of the door. The car is overall Panzer Grey and very dusty – such were the conditions in Russian in August during the 1941 summer invasion.

Stopped on a nice summer's day on a village street in northern Belgium in June 1943, this Mercedes 230 (W 143) 1939 *Tourenwagen* with a white tactical marking on its left-hand wing for a Motorized Engineering Battalion that is in yellow. The "WH" on the right-hand wing is in white. Note the full sized extra headlight mounted in the centre of the headlight bar that has not got a black out cover but has been pointed downwards to prevent glare. Lastly of interest is that under the central head light we can see that something has been scratched off the negative by the censor! I cannot imagine what could have been seen there that might have brought such action but it is of note that it proves that in this case even private photographs had gone through a censor before being made available to the owner as prints.

Here we have a *Luftwaffe* officer proudly posing with his Mercedes 230 or 260 Cabriolet B, The car is in Panzer Grey but retains its chrome bumpers. It is fitted with add-on trafficators, a wing-mounted flag pole with command pennant attached, and a Notek light. The emblem on the rear boot lid (trunk) is a very poor rendition of one of the unit badges from JG 77 – in this case a well-painted version would have been a shield with a white background with a blue bottom to it with a wild boar running along the top of the blue base, the boar being black but here the boar has become a dog's head? And the whole badge is very poorly executed. I know from other photos in this album that I purchased from an ex JG 77 ground crew (engine maintenance) member that this is indeed a car from JG 77 but without that knowledge I would not have been able to recognise this badge at all. Lastly note the mirror oddly mounted on the spare wheel retaining frame and another funny thing is that in all this snow and ice the only wheel with snow chains fitted is the spare wheel stowed on the left-hand front wing!

Both the photographs on the page are of the same Mercedes 260 Cabriolet B, 2 door, 4 seater, although this spacious car as can be seen could easily seat 5 in relative comfort. Other than the Panzer Grey overall paint job this car has no other military add-on s. The tubular bow shaped frame mounted to the bumper mounts with a central extra headlight was a factory option. Again note the mirror mounted on the spare wheel stowage retaining frame but on this occasion it is an oblong mirror not a circular one. These photos only go to demonstrate my problem with Mercedes type identification. From most angles this car would look the same as the 230 on the last page, it's only the radiator grille being seen here to be flat and not having a slight angle in it with the fold down the centre line that I could tell the two types apart. The only thing I can be totally sure of is that these two photos are of an ex-civilian requisitioned Mercedes being used as a staff car that was photographed on 11th May 1941 in the railway marshalling yards in Leipzig Germany

This Mercedes 260 Cabriolet is fitted with a flag pole on its left-hand wing and a limp sunflower can just be made out attached to it, a Notek light and add-on trafficators, one of which the soldier has his hand on whilst leaning against the car. The factory option bow shaped central headlight bar is fitted but the headlight had been lost or removed. Lastly note the wing mirror attached to the spare wheel retaining frame. This is a rare example of a late-war three-tone camouflage paint scheme, look carefully and you will see the tonal difference in some areas where small spots and lines of Red-Brown have been placed, often in the middle of patches of dark green. The base coat is Dark Sand Yellow. The photograph was taken whilst the car was still mounted on a railway flat bed and chocked in place by the wooden chocks we can see on the bottom edge of the photo. These would have been nailed to the wooden floor of the railway wagon. The date is given as 17th July 1944 but the only location information is that it is taken on a train heading east.

A Mercedes 230 soft-roofed saloon painted in overall Panzer Grey seen here close to the Russian town of Klintsy escorting a convoy made up of Kaelble and Hanomag heavy tractors, each towing a Einheits E5 trailer (standard 5 ton trailer). Note the dual wheeled axles. Sadly I have no date for the photo. It is a standard "as factory built car" with no military additions other than the paint job. Of note is the worn tread on the spare wheel and new tread on the left-hand front wheel facing the camera.

This car, that I have identified tentatively as a Mercedes 200 Cabriolet, by both its length and the flat top edge to the windscreen frame and flat radiator grille, was photographed next to a French house that was commandeered from French locals and used as officers' quarters close to the airfield at Abbeville-Drucat near the village of Drucat, France. The car has no military markings whatsoever and only the Panzer Grey paint scheme, the pair of added military style electric horns and the home-made looking wing mirror pole on the left-hand wing give it away as a military staff car. Even the soldier/officer posing next to it with one leg on the running board is dressed in what could be civilian clothing. These photos was taken on 27th March 1943. Lastly note the different tyre tread patterns on the spare tyre and left front tyre, the tyres coming from different manufacturers.

Photographed on the causeway to Mont St Michel, France, is this column of staff cars, of which at least the first two are what look to be Mercedes 260s. The car in front is painted in overall Panzer Grey with two horns added to the front bumper mounts and an added flag pole on the front left wing with a command pennant displayed, denoting it as the car belonging to a Division Commander. The photograph was taken on 29th June 1943, when the island was being used as a venue for a conference regarding the development/progress of the Atlantic Wall. Note the unit badge of a Green Heart with a white border (87th Infanterie Division) that can be seen on at least three of the cars, and the white tactical symbol for an Infantry engineering unit (Pioneers).

A poor quality but interesting photo of a Mercedes 230 soft-roofed saloon parked on a road near a bridge scheduled for crossing but demolished by the retreating BEF (British Expeditionary Force) during in May of 1940, probably on either the 12th or 13th near the Belgium town of Aalst. The road bridge in the background can be seen to have at least one span down and closer to the car we can see the support pylons of the German prefabricated engineering bridge that is in the process of being constructed. For a river this size the bridge, if not being fired on, would normally be up and running in 8 to 10 hours. The tactical symbol on the car is for a non-motorised infantry unit.

This Mercedes 230 or 260 is parked at the back of the motor maintenance shop of Munster barracks in October 1940. Of interest is that the tactical symbol is on the right-hand wing here instead of the on the left as was usual, it is in white and is the symbol for the 2nd Platoon of a Signals Company. Note all three of the headlights have canvas blackout covers and other than the paint job the car has no military additions at all. Note the car with no doors in the background, it is a rather rare BMW 309 *Kübelwagen* of 1934/35 vintage and was obsolete by 1940. If it still ran it would have no doubt still have been used as a runabout.

Stuck in a turnip field is this Mercedes 260 Cabriolet, that has been fitted with two electric military style horns and a command pennant frame that is currently displaying a command pennant of a Pioneer Regiment Commander on the right wing. On the left wing, sadly bleached out by the sun's glare, is a light blue square with a white shield with a red dancing bear on it, a variation of the city of Berlin's emblem which is where this unit was raised. Look at it hard and it can just be made out here. Lastly notice the damaged wing and the remaining unpainted chrome plated windscreen frame. The picture was taken in June 1940 in Northern Belgium.

A fully repainted in Panzer Grey Mercedes 260 sun-roof 2-door, 4 seat saloon version. The driver posing next to the car has his hand on the door handle and in front of his hand we can see the left-hand side's trafficator. Other than these means of indicating the car's intention to turn left or right I can see no more in the way of military equipment added to the vehicle. It does however have a tactical symbol on its left-hand wing above the white "WH" and it is that of a construction unit with the "*Kommandant der Pioniertruppen 14*" (Commander of the engineer troops 14) written in white under the crossed pick and shovel of the tactical symbol. The picture was taken outside the Unit Administration Block whilst stationed in the ex-French Naval Barracks in Saint-Nazaire, France in July 1943. There is a unit badge on the right-hand wing but the contrast of this type of 1940's film has made it unrecognizable.

This Mercedes 260, 2 door, 4 seat cabriolet is without doubt the most unmolested by military accoutrements of any staff car you could find. If it were not for the military occupants it might not have been recognised as a staff car at all. The car is as it left the factory, still in its high gloss black overall finish with chrome plated hardware and trim. The photo was taken in October 1940 somewhere in Germany but I have no more detailed information than that.

The only officer everyone likes, this Mercedes 260 cabriolet belongs to an infantry regiment's paymaster as denoted by the yellow tactical symbol on the left-hand wing below the white "WH". The car is in overall Panzer Grey but still sports its original chrome plated window frames, all left unpainte, as are the two electric horns mounted on the front bumper. However the most interesting thing about this car is that it has on the left-hand wing a command pennant frame with a command pennant in it, with a cover over it and on the right-hand wing a flag pole with another command pennant mounted on it. The paymaster is seen talking to the unit's adjutant on his horse. The photo was taken on Sunday afternoon, 29th October 1939.

In a classic "look at what have I got" pose we have a group of young *Wehrmacht* officers posing with their new toy, a Mercedes 230 or 260 cabriolet. Note the young officer sitting on the running board with the front door open, holding the key up to the camera. The car is resplendent in a brand new coat of Panzer Grey – note how dark it looks in its as-new just applied condition. It would soon fade down a bit and with the accumulation of dust appear much the same as the other cars in this book. Just visible in the background is a small Borgward 3 wheeler, the P400, a ubiquitous vehicle that was made in the thousands yet hardly ever photographed as it just was not as sexy as a new Merc! This photo was taken in May 1939 in Koblenz, Germany

An interesting pose is struck by this soldier for a photo to send home. He is pretending to fire an MP 34 manufactured by Waffenfabrik Steyr between 1929 and 1940; he is standing behind a Mercedes 260 cabriolet. We have in this view a close-up of the waxed cotton headlight blackout covers and the spare wheel stowage bracket mounted rear view mirror. Annoying as it is, I know I have seen this unit marking before but I can't find any reference to it. It is also frustrating that it obviously has a word painted on to the radiator grille but the padded cold weather cover, although open, obstructs the first half of the word. The only thing I can add for sure is that the photo was taken on a farm on 2nd July 1941.

This Mercedes 260 belongs to the *Luftwaffe* and is seen driving along a picturesque road in eastern France close to the Luxemburg border in 1941. This is odd for me to understand but this photograph was taken whilst this group are on holiday! They have not gone home but are doing a driving holiday in eastern France, a recently occupied country of a recently defeated enemy whist at war with their allies? The car is overall Panzer Grey with added trafficators, two electric horns and a hand operated spot light mounted on the driver's side "A" pillar.

This Mercedes 230 Cabriolet 4 door, 4 seater is only recently requisitioned and has just been issued to the motor pool for militarization. We can see one of the mechanics with a paint brush at the front of the car about to paint either the number plate radiator grille or bumpers Panzer Grey. Note he is using a brush – most cars were repainted this way as spray booths and indeed spray guns were not so widespread and available in the 1940s. I have pictures of German vehicles being painted with mops, rags and even a broom in my collection. This beautiful car was photographed for the last time in its glorious factory finish on 16th July 1940 in Hannover, Germany.

A most interesting photograph here of what I believe to be a Mercedes 200 Cabriolet 2-door 2-seater that is being towed in whilst being loaded on board an Einheits E3 trailer (standard 3 ton trailer). There were several different designs accepted as E3s, this one is of the Borgward type and was offered as an extra in conjunction with their 3 ton trucks before the war. They were made in the thousands during the war for the *Wehrmacht* and in particular for the Organisation Todt, the German government run civil and military engineering arm. The car has been well used and its Panzer Grey paint, that was applied without any form of service preparation, is cracking off the high gloss finish below that looks to have been the very attractive Sky Blue that was one of the colours available as standard from Mercedes direct as a new purchase pre-war. The trailer has in the past been used as a medical wagon and half the white circle and red cross is still visible. The tactical marking on the truck's rear is that of a motorized transport company and the whole ensemble was photographed on their way back to Lviv, in the Ukraine, on 4th April 1943.

Seen outside a municipal building in Warsaw, Poland, on 19th December 1940, is this very nice looking Mercedes 230 with only two extra horns and a flag pole with a command pennant attached added to its immaculate factory finish of dark blue chassis and wings with a gull grey body with chrome plated hardware and trim. This was another of the standard factory civilian finishes. The motorcycle behind the car is a BMW R12 with a sidecar.

This Mercedes 260 Cabriolet has the look of a spray-painted finish to its Panzer Grey coat, giving it a satin like appearance. The photo was taken amongst the tree-lined roads of the officers' married quarters residential area. Just one such area in the vast complex that was the Frankfurt military barracks complex in the 1930s. This photo was taken in May 1940.

Mercedes 260 & 320 *Kübelwagen*

Before the war the German military asked several companies to produce an off-road military car that have generically become known as "*Kübelwagens*" (bucket seated cars). The Mercedes offering was named after the town where it was made – Stuttgart, Germany. This Mercedes Stuttgart is seen having just had a wheel change whilst on exercise in the Frankfurt area of Germany in July 1939. The car is overall Panzer Grey in colour. The car itself is in very good condition; note the towing hooks bolted onto the front wings and the rolled up canvas door aperture covering belted to the front of the car's "A" pillar.

The Mercedes-Benz cars that found their way into military service as were illustrated and discussed in the previous section header also had many of their various chassis types used in the manufacture of military specific vehicles mostly as open-topped, bucket-seated without metal doors and only with canvas door curtains (that were rarely used in service). The cars were used for troop transport but occasionally bodywork for specialist tasks such as radio communication cars or even ambulances was fitted. The photographs in this section are of such vehicles. Their manufacturing history ran concurrently with their civilian counterparts, but they were manufactured in much lower numbers.

This Mercedes Stuttgart is part of a demonstration team that was to undertake a dummy form of attack demonstration in a school playing field for the education of the children. The Nazi Party were experts at this type of propaganda to draw the public into a national feeling that they the civilians were part of one national force in conjunction with the armed forces. The photograph is dated 12th October 1938.

Yet another demonstration during a school visit by the army. This time it was in June 1938 at a small school in the village of Schkeuditz, Germany, near Leipzig. It's now a mid-sized town. Note the pattern of cut-outs in the wheel – this was peculiar to the Mercedes type and can be seen on both their trucks and cars and sometimes its the only means of identifying a vehicle as a Mercedes type. Note in this June of 1938 photo no blackout covers are required on the headlights.

This Mercedes Stuttgart is seen at the Lüneburg training grounds on 9th December 1938. Of note is that this is the only photo I have of a white-washed vehicle from the pre-war period. I had previously thought that this practice did not come into play until the winter of 1940/41 in Russia, but no here it is in evidence in Germany in 1938! The wooden caravan in the background is one of many different types and styles of command caravans that saw service in the early war years. Lastly notice the tow cable wrapped around the bumper supports, an indication no doubt as the reliability of these early off road car types, and that the car is fitted with a very early Notek light that only started to become available during trials from late 1937 and in small numbers at first.

Here we have another Mercedes Stuttgart, but this one is a rarity to be sure. It is fitted with steel doors – very few were so equipped! It is seen driving through a Polish village during the 1939 invasion. Sadly I have no more information on this photo, but of interest is the detail it offers of the spade stowage that would normally be hidden by the stowed spare wheel.

This Mercedes Stuttgart is seen whilst driving up to its starting position for the invasion of Luxemburg & France though the Ardennes forest region that covers that area of all three countries. The photo is dated 8th May 1940 and proves that at least some of these early off-road types saw service in the west. Of interest here is that the spare wheel still has a snow chain fitted and that the windscreen is folded down and covered with a folded blanket, to avoid any reflected glare being spotted by an enemy.

Opposite page, bottom: A parting gesture as these officers give a higher ranking office a farewell salute. The Mercedes he is leaving in is the majestic Mercedes 320, both wider and longer than the 260 & 230 but still retaining much the same overall look due to many of the same style elements being employed. This photo was taken at a commandeered chateau somewhere along the river Loire valley, France, on 12th May 1941. Note the command pennant on the left front wing and the rolled up log fascine, that does not look as if it has ever been used, tucked down in between the engine cover and the right-hand wing,

Mercedes 320

This Mercedes model W142 type 320 Cabriolet (C) is a four-door, 6-seater and it is seen here being refuelled at a civilian garage somewhere in the suburbs of Essen, Germany during September of 1939. The car is painted overall Panzer Grey and has been fitted with a driver's side hand operated spot light.

Mercedes 320, W142

The Mercedes-Benz 320 was manufactured between 1937 through 1942 when like all other civilian car type production ceased. It was produced at the Mercedes plant in Stuttgart, Germany in 4 different variants, the 320 W142/I, 320 W142/II, 320 W142/III and 320 W142/IV. The "W" Prefix denotes the factory works number and it is often the factory works number that is used to precisely identify a Mercedes type as they of reuse the type number a common confusing trait with many German car manufacturers i.e the Mercedes 320 could refer to either 1937-42 style of car or indeed the Mercedes 320 series that was manufactured from 1993 and is still in production today, both very different cars! It should be noted that all of the 1937–42 320's were also in varying numbers purchased directly by the German military with either little or no changes in their production specification. Many of the military purchases were fitted in the factory with weapon clips/holders for MP 38/40's, extra headlamps and/or a Notek light but not all.

The Mercedes 320 W142/I was produced from 1937 until terminated in 1938. It was available in two type variations, both with a wheel base of 2.88 meters (short wheel base). It was available as either a 2-door, 3-seat a soft top cabriolet or a coupé-bodied equivalent with a hard top removable roof. It was powered by a 3,208 cc side-valve petrol engine which gave the car a top speed of over 80 mph.

The Mercedes 320 W142/II, was produced from 1937 until terminated in 1938. It was available with a large number of body types but all had a wheel base of 3.3 meters (long wheelbase). Four different cabriolet variations,
- Cabriolet (A): A two-door two/three seater
- Cabriolet (B): A two-door 4-seater
- Cabriolet (C): A four-door 6-seater
- Cabriolet (D): A four-door 4-seater
- Two other soft top variations were also available:
- A six seat "torpedo-bodied" Tourer
- A two door 2 seat roadster (sports car)
- A Limousine hard top with four doors six seats in three rows, fashioned by Pullman,
- and lastly the standard hard top saloon with four doors and four seats.
- The W142/II was powered by the same engine with same drive train as the W141/1.

The Mercedes 320 W142/III was produced from 1937 until terminated in 1939; it utilized the same short wheelbase chassis as the W142/1 and known in Mercedes as the *WehrmachtsKübelwagen*. It was purposely designed for the military, one of its main identification features is that unlike any other type of 320 W142 variant, it had a bar fitted across its radiator, fixed to both fenders onto which headlights were fitted. It also featured four doors and a canvas tilt. Mercedes redesigned the engine and commenced production of an increased cylinder bore, to the block producing an engine now with 3.405cc. and also lowered its compression in order for the engine to more readily accept the lower grade synthetic fuel that was to become more common in the fuel supply as the war went on

The Mercedes 320 W142/IV was produced from 1938 until terminated in 1942; it utilized the same larger capacity engine as the W142/III. It came in two body styles: a 4-door 4-seat soft top cabriolet, and a 4-door hard top saloon. Although a civilian design, many of this type production run were purchased directly by the military and civilian government for high ranking officials transports.

In all Mercedes produced 7,017 W142's of all variants, 4,326 of the 3.208 cc engined W142/I and W142/II/s, and 885 of the W142IV's and 1,806 of the military W142/III's powered by the 3,405 cc rebored engine.

Opposite page, bottom: A beautiful overall gloss black and chrome Mercedes 320. Just by looking at the worn tyres we can see this is not a new car, but it has been cleaned and polished and positively shines. The NSKK Standartenführer leans casually on the car for this hero shot keepsake. Such luxury cars were often to be seen in the possession of these political supremos of Nazi Party organisations. The photo was taken in the bus station area of Nuremberg National Arena during a rehearsal for the parade for Hitler's Birthday address to be held on his birthday – 20th April. This practice was held on 18th April 1939.

Note NSKK (German: Nationalsozialistisches Kraftfahrkorps, NSKK) National Socialist Motor Corps was a paramilitary organization of the Nazi Party.*

Above: This photograph was taken in the garage area of the French Tank Barracks in Saumur, France, which the Germans garrisoned from September 1940. This Mercedes 320 is being looked over by its new owners. It's no wonder that they are so enthusiastic, as I doubt any of the group had ever seen such a luxury car before and they are determined to enjoy the experience. According to the comment on the rear of the photo one of the group thought it was the best car he had ever seen and "it drove like riding a cloud". This car was photographed on 3rd August 1941.
NOTE: Saumur is now the home of the French Tank Museum and has a fantastic collection of exhibits. I can't recommend a visit strongly enough!

Another Mercedes 320, being used as the backdrop for posed photo to send home. This car is still in its original factory gloss black and chrome finish. The photo was taken at an appropriated house in Berlin and now is the home to two *Wehrmacht* officers and their families. There is a poignant note on the rear of the photo that tells us the house used to belong to a Jewish family and celebrates their eviction (and also anticipating their demise in a written sentiment I will not reproduce here). Note the trunk on the rear of the car, it is an actual trunk and could easily be removed in the manner of a suitcase in a car boot today.

This photograph was taken on 8th June 1940, only 3 days after the last evacuation from Dunkirk of over 26,000 of the French rear guard troops on the 4th. Dunkirk became a must-see place for as many Germans who could finagle a way to visit it during the next few weeks. Here a Mercedes 320 with two German soldiers and two Nazi party officials take a tour of the beach front. The car has been repainted overall Panzer Grey and is fitted with the factory custom made cover for the folded down roof and a Notek light mounted on top of the triangular bar that still also retains the factory-fitted option of a third headlight.

Photographed parked alongside a road next to an office block in the industrial suburbs of Brussels, Belgium, on 16th May 1940 we can see a Mercedes 320 in overall Panzer Grey. It is fitted with waxed cloth blackout covers, a padded cold weather radiator guard and a small spot light on the light mounting bar fitted between the two front wings in front of the radiator. This car also sports a flag pole on the right-hand front wing that has a *Wehrmacht* Division Commander's pennant attached to it.

Another Mercedes 320 in my favourite factory paint scheme of Dark Sky Blue front and back wings with Gull Grey body panels, complete with chromed hardware and trim. Note the black factory-fitted rubber mat on the running board held on with a chrome frame. The small notch that is visible in the outer edge of the running board is where the car's jacking point is located. The car is fitted with an unusual command pennant but sadly not enough of it is in frame of the shot to enable positive recognition.

This is the same car as seen on the previous page, only here in a good quality front view. We can see now that the car has a Notek light on its left-hand side front wing and small flag poles on both front wings. Note the odd placement of a command pennant that denotes an infantry HQ vehicle on the left-hand side of the bumper next to the left nudge bar. The tactical symbol above the "WH" and below the Notek light is that of a brigade commander. The Black shield with White border and an animal head in the centre of the black background painted in white on the right-hand wing I do not recognise. The head does look a bit like a terrier dog but could be any number of animals – the artist does not have a high degree of talent!

Opposite page, top: A convoy of high ranking officers are returning to their cars following a photo opportunity with Reich Marshal Hermann Goering at the coastal radar and defensive system built at "Cap Gris Nez" near Sangatte, France, The photo-op was the now famous photo shoot of Goering watching the *Luftwaffe* launch its largest raid to date on Britain. Behind the German-assembled Chrysler (Chrysler US shipped kits of parts to their German subsidiary) is a Mercedes 320 in full view. The car is finished in overall gloss black & chrome and is fitted with a Notek light and two flag poles, one on each front wing. The pennant mounted on the left is indistinguishable, but the one on the right is that of the commander-in-chief of an army group, in this case Army Group "C" under *Generalfeldmarschall* Wilhelm Ritter von Leeb. Strangely the command pennant is repeated on a smaller scale over the front bumper.

Taken outside the main entrance to a hospital in Brussels, Belgium, is this Mercedes 320 in overall Panzer Grey. I can see no military additions other than the paint job. Note on the bonnet (engine cover) the large white circle with a red cross inside. Painted in this location on the top of the body for protection from aerial attack. Worthy of note is that in 1943 the Germans felt no need to paint the Red Cross anywhere on the sides of this car. The photograph is dated 27th May 1943.

Here I am taking the photographer's word for it that, as stated on the rear of the picture, this is a Mercedes 320 4-door 6-seater that he photographed outside Leipzig railway station on 21st July 1942. Whilst this is a blurry shot I have included it as to me it epitomizes the image that a big Mercedes invokes as it glides by at speed. The car is overall gloss black with chrome hardware and trim, with only command pennants fitted on both the left and right-hand front wings by way of military additions.

Another Mercedes 320 4 door, 6 seater cabriolet seen here parked on a road somewhere in north-eastern Holland during September 1942. Its nicely weathered down Panzer Grey paint has mellowed to a mid-grey colour and the addition of a dust coat makes the car blend in quite well with its surroundings. Fitted as military extras to this Mercedes are a full width heated windscreen, a driver's side hand operated spotlight, also command pennant holding frame on the right-hand front wing and a flag pole on the left-hand wing. The flag on the right is covered up but the pennant on the left is fully visible and denotes the car as belonging to a general of the *Heer* (army) and indeed a colonel is seen to be posing next to the car. Lastly the tactical symbol in white on the left-hand wing is that of a Group Commander's Headquarters vehicle, attached to a Motorized Corps Headquarters.

Mercedes 540

Photographs of the 540K in service are very rare, as was the vehicle itself as only a few hundred ever constructed. This Mercedes 540K is seen in Gent, Belgium, during the winter of 1942/43. It has been repainted overall Panzer Grey and has had two electric horns added to the front bumper. The car, belonging to a high ranking *Luftwaffe* officer, has been involved in a small accident by sliding on the ice into the side of a truck. Evidently the bump was enough to crack the distributor cap and hence the car is immobile – so the text on the photograph's rear tells me. There are two markings on the left-hand side front wing, a yellow dot and below that a white ring that I have found a number of different meanings to, from a signals unit (telephones) to an anti-tank symbol. Sadly none of the identities that I have found are very likely to have been issued with such a prestigious vehicle! These cars were for very senior officers not for lower ranking field officers.

Mercedes 500K & 540K, W24

The Mercedes-Benz 540K works number of W24 was manufactured between 1936 until 1940 with some chassis still having body work fitted as late as 1944 by special order of the German High command for which these cars were ultimately intended, they were all built at Mercedes in its Sinddelfingen plant were Mercedes had a separate custom bodywork shop employing over 1500 people, the 540K was first introduced to the public at the 1936 Paris Motor Show.

This car was always only ever intended to be for the financial elite and very high ranking government officials the 500K & 540k was really to all intents and purposes a custom built car with only 342 500K's and 419 540K's being produced in all and of that total of 743, 70 chassis were not finished by Mercedes but were sent to other body builders and coachworks worldwide by the individual customer who had purchase it. The 540K essentially differed from the 500K by the construction of its cassis the 500K's chassis was fabricated with tradition box frame girder style design. However influenced by Mercedes design successes with their racing cars of the late 1930's (the "Silver Arrows") the 540K's chassis was constructed utilizing oval tubes it was much lighter yet still as structurally sound. This, combined with the large percentage of custom body work, makes identification between the 500 and 540K very difficult.

The standard power plant for the 500K & 540K was the Mercedes straight 8-cylinder engine of 5,401 cc that was so powerful it could propel these vehicles at speeds of up to 110 mph, which was truly astounding in those days for any car, let alone one as large as the 500K/540K's. Whilst many of these cars were fitted with varying styles of custom bodies there were a few standard body designs that were manufactured in appreciable numbers such as the 4-door 4-seater cabriolets various touring and saloon cars.

Production figures break down the body work types as follows:
- 296 Cabriolets (B) Four Door, Four Seats & Two Side Windows, with 3.29 metre wheelbase
- 122 Cabriolets (C) Four Door, Four Seats & Three Side Windows, with 3.29 v wheelbase
- 116 Cabriolets (A) Two Door, Four Seats, with 2.98 metre wheelbase

- 70 Chassis with body work supplied & fitted by third party body/coach works world-wide.
- 58 Roadsters
- 29 Saloons with 2 doors (mainly 540K)
- 28 Open Touring Car (offener Tourenwagen)
- 23 Saloons with 4 doors (mainly 500K)
- 12 Coupés
- 6 Motorway Cruisers (Autobahn-kurier) Mercedes 500K & 540K, W24

This car was always only ever intended to be for the financial elite and very high ranking government officials the 500K & 540k was really to all intense and purposes a custom built car with only 342 500K's and 419 540K's being produced in all and of that total of 743, 70 chassis were not finished by Mercedes but were sent to other body builders Coachworks worldwide by the individual customer who had purchase it. The 540K essentially differed from the 500K by the construction of its cassis the 500K's chassis was fabricated with tradition box frame girder style design however influenced by Mercedes design successes with their racing cars of the late 1930's (the "Silver Arrows") the 540K's chassis was constructed utilizing oval tubes it was much lighter yet still as structurally sound. This combined with the large percentage of custom body work makes identification between the 500 and 540K very difficult.

This and opposite page: A sadly battered Mercedes 540K, one of the most luxurious cars made anywhere in the world in the late 1930s or early 1940s. The car is seen left at the roadside awaiting recovery following its accident. It must have spun into whatever it hit as it has received damage to all sides. The car belonged to the divisional commander of the of the 3rd Infanterie Division (motorised) which became a Panzer Grenadier division in 1943, as denoted by the tactical symbol on the right front wing in white and the unit badge of the division in yellow on the left-had front wing above the white "WH" for the *Wehrmacht*. The car is in its original factory finish of gloss black chassis and wings with body panels in cream, with chrome plated hardware and trim.

Well it is still a staff car, but as is clearly indicated by the large white painted Star in a white circle, this Mercedes is now in the hands of the Allies and is parked outside a barn that has been turned into a garage, behind a rather up-market house in the suburbs of Bielefeld, Germany. This has been confiscated by the Allies as a temporary headquarters. The car is still in its Panzer Grey & chrome finish but has had its German unit and tactical marking painted over in Olive Drab, with new identification numbers added in white both on the newly painted Olive Drab areas of the wings and on the engine bonnet lid along the side hinge line.

Here we have a either a Mercedes 500 or 540K photographed in Berlin on 18th April 1941. It is still in its factory finish of overall gloss black with chrome plated hardware and trim. It is fitted with the factory option of an added cloth cover for the folded down roof and also of note is the unusual position in which the front number plate is fitted, above the bumper to the right of the radiator grille.

Mercedes G4

A rare factory photograph from my collection, as over 99% of it is made up of private photographs from ordinary soldiers. This photo must have been acquired by one such soldier and added to his album. It is of course an excellent side view of the iconic Mercedes G4 Cabriolet. Seen here in one of the factory standard finishes of gloss black wings and chassis with cream body panels and tons of chrome plated accessories. A four door 6-seater, 6-wheeled monster of a car.

A very rare conversion indeed, included here due to it once having been a staff car but needs for a recovery vehicle must have drastically overwhelmed the need for a statement piece of show art. This Mercedes G4 is seen to have been converted into a recovery vehicle surely a one-off! The car/recovery truck was photographed in Turin, Italy, in August 1944, as this repair and maintenance unit of the reserve Jager Battalion 38, part of the 189th Reserve Division, that drove northeast to either take part in the 2nd Battle for France or be diverted towards the Italian front.

Members of the general staff inspect elements of the 10th Panzer division near the Polish border on 28th August 1939, just days before the invasion began on September the 1st. Amongst those officers in the car are *Generaloberst* Fedor von Bock and General Günther von Kluge, later promoted to field-marshal. The car is still in its factory finish of gloss black chassis and wings with cream body panels. The tanks seen here are mostly Panzer I Ausf Bs but there is one Panzer II Ausf B in the line-up as well, 2nd from the right.

Mercedes G4, W31

The Mercedes G4, Works number W31, has become the iconic German Staff car yet in reality Mercedes only ever made 57 of them with only 11 being supplied to the Military. The rest were reserved for use by high ranking NAZI officials. This 6x4 behemoth of a car was produced from 1934 until production was terminated in 1939. Production was never a priority with only 11 being produced between 1934 and 1937, 16 more in 1937 to 1938 and the final 30 being manufactured between 1938 and the end of 1939. The first 11 G4s were powered by a 5,018 cc Mercedes engine, the next batch of 16 were powered by a 5,252cc engine and the last batch of 30 by a 5,401 cc engine. Whilst their service life was mainly just being used in the early years for state visits or parades, it is known that at least one was converted in to a fire engine sometime in 1944. As you will see in this publication I have a photo in my collection of a Mercedes G4 that has been converted into a recovery vehicle in March of 1944, that no doubt was of more use to the German army than an oversized fuel guzzling statement piece. Most of the G4s produced were open-topped tourers but a few were completed with enclosed hard top type saloon bodies. Yet this very low production vehicle has become the most common to survive by manufactured quantity percentage. With only 57 produced, 3 are known to be in museums or private collections today. I guess mostly due to the amount of film footage in surviving newsreels of them in various parades being used to transport both German and foreign heads of state during visits to Germany they have become, as already stated, the most iconic of the Mercedes car family. In reality, they were far from the best or the most useful to the German military from the Mercedes catalogue. The fact that most G4s featured armoured floors, armoured body work and bullet proof windows all round yet were left open-topped but for a soft canvas fold-down roof says it all.